The Prioress' Prologue and Tale

D0858835

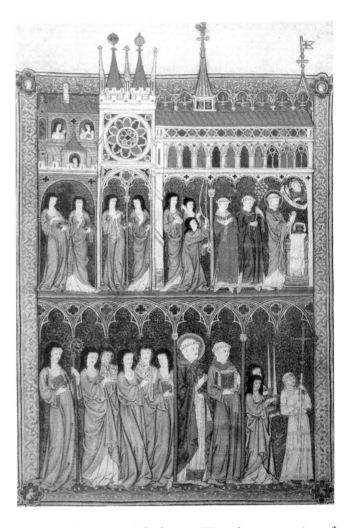

Scenes of convent life from a French manuscript of about 1300. Although it was more usually carried by an abbess, the crosier was carried by the prioress in certain orders and foundations.

AMBRIDGE

The Prioress' Prologue and Tale

Selected Tales from Chaucer

Edited by James Winny

CAMBRIDGE
UNIVERSITY PRESS

University Printing House, Cambridge CB2 8BS, United Kingdom

Cambridge University Press is part of the University of Cambridge.

It furthers the University's mission by disseminating knowledge in the pursuit of education, learning and research at the highest international levels of excellence.

www.cambridge.org

Information on this title: www.cambridge.org/9781316615621

© Cambridge University Press 1975, 2008, 2016

First published 1975

Reissued 2008, 2016

A catalogue record for this publication is available from the British Library

ISBN 978-1-316-61562-1 paperback

Frontispiece © World History Archive/Alamy Stock Photo (image from a La Somme le Roi manuscript at the British Library)
Cover illustration © Shutterstock

Contents

FOR MY DAUGHTER
BEATRICE LOUISE

Introduction

The religious legend told by the Prioress forms part of the longest
continuous run of tales in the Canterbury collection, comprising
six very dissimilar stories. The Shipman speaks first, and his fabliau
of wifely deception is followed by *The Prioress' Tale*. Next Chaucer
himself is called forward and begins the wretched tale of *Sir
Thopas*, which he is not allowed to finish. For this failure he
substitutes the long prose story *Melibee*, a tedious moral discourse
which the Host hears out with rueful feelings, wishing that his
ferocious wife Goodelief could have heard it. Then comes the
Monk's depressing recital of tragedies, cut short by the Knight; and
the section ends with the lively tale of Chauntecleer and Pertelote,
narrated by the Nun's Priest. In this varied group of stories *The
Prioress' Tale* has the disadvantage of being very short. Apart from
some of the fragmentary stories left unfinished by Chaucer, it is in
fact the shortest of *The Canterbury Tales*,[1] but it is generally
regarded as one of the most accomplished and craftsmanlike of the
poet's works. The reaction of the pilgrim audience indicates its
power. At the end of the tale they remain silent and awed, and,
until the Host shatters this sober mood with a joke, the holiday
spirit of the pilgrimage is suspended.

  Why Chaucer should have placed *The Prioress' Tale* between
the Shipman's fabliau and the 'rym dogerel' of *Sir Thopas* is
uncertain, but we should assume that the order of the tales is
purposeful and not random. Some of the stories seem to be
arranged so that they reflect ironically upon each other. *The
Miller's Tale* parodies the ideal of love expressed in *The Knight's Tale*
which precedes it, and *The Clerk's Tale* presents a view of wifely
submission much at odds with the outlook of *The Wife's Prologue*,

---

[1] The tale itself amounts to only 202 lines. For comparison, both *The Miller's Tale* and *The
Nun's Priest's Tale* are over 600 lines.

where Alisoun sets out her defiant opinions about the sovereignty of women. Chaucer's original intention in linking the stories of the Prioress and the Shipman must have been related to a scheme later abandoned, for at first it was the Wife of Bath who told the story now assigned to the Shipman.[1] This arrangement would have contrasted the literary tastes of the Wife and the Prioress, each of whom reveals herself through her choice of entertainment. Later, when the Wife's story of a cheated husband was transferred to the Shipman, the contrast took a different form; for in making one of its characters a licentious monk, *The Shipman's Tale* expresses a worldly and knowing attitude towards the Church which finds no sympathetic echo in *The Prioress' Tale*. At a time when all clergy were committed to sexual abstinence, the lapses of a priest or monk provided the storyteller with a ready joke; and several of Chaucer's ecclesiastical pilgrims are made comic by this means. From her portrait in *The General Prologue* it appears that the Prioress's religious vocation is as doubtful as the Monk's; but the Prioress justifies herself by telling a tale whose religious sincerity reduces the audience to a solemn silence.

Like the rest of *The Canterbury Tales*, the story told by the Prioress was not original to Chaucer, though he probably developed and improved a current legend whose exact nature is hard to determine. Since the legend is known to have existed in over thirty different forms, that fact is not surprising. The most that can be said about the likely source of Chaucer's tale is that it resembled some versions of one of the three main variants of the same story, all concerning a small boy or chorister who is murdered by Jews and miraculously enabled to continue singing by the power of the Virgin. In the first, a little boy who has learnt the *Gaude Maria* at school, and who sings the anthem as he passes

---

[1] See Robinson, *The Complete Works of Geoffrey Chaucer*, Oxford 1957, VII, 11–19, where the narrator speaks as a married woman. The only other women among the pilgrims are nuns.

through the streets, is killed by a Jew who takes offence at the anthem's slighting reference to his people. He buries the body inside his house, making the floor level to disguise the grave. After a sleepless night the boy's mother begins a search for her son, which continues for several days, and at last comes to the street where he was murdered. There she hears her son singing *Gaude Maria*, and an astonished crowd begins to ransack the neighbouring houses until they reach his hidden burial place. As the voice seems to come out of the earth, they dig and find the boy alive and well, but with scars on his head where he was struck with an axe. The child explains that when he reached the Jew's house he felt sleepy and dozed off. After a long sleep he was aroused by the Virgin, who scolded him for not singing her anthem and told him to begin at once: he obeyed, with the consequence which his rescuers know.

The second variant also ends with the murdered boy restored to life by the power of the Virgin, but no mother figures in the story. The child is now a chorister who assists the priest during service; he sings not in the street but only in church, and the Jews who take his life have a much less convincing reason for hating him. Again he is miraculously brought back to life, not where he was murdered but in the church, where he is found singing as before. It is a weaker form of the legend, chiefly because by omitting the mother the story loses the episode of her search and the astonishing discovery of the boy singing underground. Like the first variant, however, it ends happily with the child alive and unharmed by his experience.

Chaucer followed a third variant, in which the murdured boy is not restored to life. Considered simply on its merits as a story, this seems preferable to the other variants because it introduces several new features. The guilty Jews are seized and punished for their crime, the boy's continued singing is made more wonderful by his death wound, and his mother's grief adds a level of pathetic feeling to the tale. In this variant as in the other two, the murder is committed by Jews incensed by the singing of a Christian anthem in their ghetto, so the child can be considered a martyr to his faith. This adds another element of interest to the story, very plausibly associated with the Prioress, who expresses an ecstasy of religious joy over this juvenile 'martir sowded to virginitee'.[1] A further marvellous feature is provided by the token placed in the murdered boy's mouth by the Virgin, which enables him to continue chanting her praises. In a version of the tale reprinted by R. D. French,[2] the token is a lily inscribed with golden letters; in Chaucer's version it is a small pearl. When it is removed, the singing stops and the boy is given a martyr's funeral. The moving passage in *The Prioress' Tale,* where the boy himself explains how the pearl was placed on his tongue, implicitly asking the abbot to remove it, has the ring of a Chaucerian embellishment of the legend. It also allows us to sense Madam Eglantine's emotional involvement in her tale.

Her evident sincerity of purpose is somewhat unexpected. *The General Prologue* shows the Prioress to be at least as interested in courtly manners and deportment as in her religious responsibilities, and suggests that her lapdogs mean more to her than the poor and wretched. This long and closely observant portrait provides the first clear sign of Chaucer's satirical intentions in the poem. The three pilgrims described at the beginning of the human catalogue – Knight, Squire and Yeoman – are treated respectfully, as a group of men dedicated to an ideal of loyal service, whether to a feudal overlord or to the chivalric code. The three who follow – Prioress, Monk and Friar – have dedicated themselves to a similar ideal, but they have found its demands too austere and exacting, and have backed away towards

---

[1] 'Martyr wedded to virginity'. The Prioress's pride in her modish singing of divine service, 'entuned in hir nose ful semely', suggests another link with the hero of the tale.

2 *A Chaucer Handbook*, New York 1947, pp. 238–42.

a less arduous form of life. In a blandly satirical line, Chaucer
indicates how the Prioress has avoided meeting her spiritual
obligations:

> And al was conscience and tendre herte.
>
> > *(The General Prologue, 150)*

We might mistake this for a complimentary remark, but
'conscience' means sensibility, that delicate acuteness of feeling
expected of a well-bred lady, and which the Prioress displays as
evidence of her social origins. Moreover the comment rounds off
an account of her concern not with suffering humanity but for
trapped mice and mistreated lapdogs. We remember this
sentimental regard for small and helpless creatures when the
Prioress tells her story about a seven-year-old boy killed by the
Jews whom he enrages by singing a Christian anthem in their
ghetto. The adjective 'litel' establishes itself as a recurrent note in
the narrative, underlining the speaker's ready compassion towards
the fatherless boy, whose pitiful death cannot suppress his heartfelt
singing to the Virgin.

In other respects we may feel that the tale does not properly
represent the Prioress of *The General Prologue*. When Chaucer
notices how she

> peyned hire to countrefete cheere
> Of court   *(The General Prologue, 139–40)*

he puts a finger on an aspect of the Prioress's behaviour that is
plainly spurious. She is at pains to 'countrefete' or imitate courtly
manners because they are not in fact natural to her. Like the
Cockney French accent which betrays her middle-class
background, and like the elegant tablemanners which the narrator
describes in such admiring detail, they have been learned and
practised so that the Prioress can pass among the undiscriminating

as a lady. Much of Chaucer's satire in the portrait is directed at the charming dissimulation which just falls short of its aim and exposes itself; but her tale gives no indication that its courtly manner is assumed. Not all the tales can be expected to throw further light on the pilgrims concerned. Chaucer's chief responsibility was to the story itself, not with the disclosures which it might contain about the character of the teller. So the Prioress is allowed to speak with a dignity she just fails to grasp in *The General Prologue*, and without the touch of absurdity which makes her portrait so captivating.

Her personal dignity and wish to be respected, 'digne of reverence', are recognised by the Host, a discerning judge of character who guides the pilgrims and generally determines the order of their tales. At the end of *The Shipman's Tale* he bursts into noisy approval of a story hardly fit for nuns' ears, prefaced by a characteristically doubtful scrap of Latin:

> 'Wel seyd, by *corpus dominus!*' quod oure Hoost,
> 'Now longe moote thou saille by the cost,
> Sire gentil maister, gentil marineer!'   (vii, 435–7)

Whether by birth or behaviour, 'gentil' the Shipman is not, but the Host's enthusiasm is carrying him to extremes. As he rounds off his congratulations and looks about him to see who should tell the next story, his eye falls on the Prioress; and his raucous back-slapping is instantly replaced by an elaborately polite submission, spoken 'as curteisly as it had been a mayde':

> 'My lady Prioresse, by youre leve,
> So that I wiste I sholde you nat greve,
> I wolde demen that ye tellen sholde
> A tale next, if so were that ye wolde.

Now wol ye vouche sauf, my lady deere?'[1]

This tiptoeing approach to the Host's proposal might conceal a grain of mockery, but if so the Prioress does not sense it; and as she acquiesces we feel her glowing inwardly at the Host's unusual deference: the only pilgrim apart from the Knight whom he addresses without roughness or banter.

After the 'murie wordes' which separate *The Shipman's Tale* from *The Prioress' Prologue*, Chaucer reverts from the decasyllabic couplet of his final style to rhyme royal, a 7-line stanza which he had employed throughout the middle part of his career. The poems written in rhyme royal, which include *The Parlement of Foules*, the tales of the Clerk and the Monk – both written before the conception of *The Canterbury Tales* – and *Troilus and Criseyde*, share a common concern with ideal forms of behaviour, lofty subject matter and deeply affecting emotions. The ideals are generally those of *fine amour* or of nobility; the subject matter usually avoids contact with everyday affairs; and the feelings often invite the reader to weep in sympathy with undeserved distress or grief. This generalisation must be qualified by admitting that Chaucer seldom allows unearthly sentiments and ideals to pass unchallenged by the voice of commonsense. Such a challenge is explicitly made by the lower-class birds in *The Parlement of Foules*, who protest indignantly at the impractical principles adopted by the noble eagles at mating time, which threaten to delay the proceedings interminably. But despite this conflict, a large part of Chaucer's imaginative interest is held by courtly ideas which are not discredited by the pragmatism of workaday experience; and the style of these poems reflects his involvement with a realm of thought nobler and more beautiful than reality provides. Where

---

[1] 'Dear lady, with your permission, if I were sure that it wouldn't embarrass you in any way, I might suggest that you should tell the next story, if you would be so very kind. Could you possibly agree to do this, dear madam?'

the decasyllabic couplets of the late work allow him to represent
the movement of colloquial speech with very little hindrance
from poetic form, in rhyme royal Chaucer must organise language
into a much more complex structure that is consciously artificial
and literary. The passage beginning 'Wel seyd, by *corpus dominus!*' is
poetry and not a direct transcript of popular speech, but in several
ways it is much closer to spoken English than Chaucer's
characteristic writing in rhyme royal. The following stanza
describes how, after Criseyde's departure from Troy, her lover
Troilus returns to the deserted house where she had lived:

> Therwith, whan he was war and gan biholde
> How shet was every window of the place,
> As frost, him thoughte, his herte gan to colde;
> For which with chaunged dedlich pale face
> Withouten word, he forthby gan to pace,
> And, as God wolde, he gan so faste ride
> That no wight of his contenance espide.
>
> (*Troilus and Criseyde*, v, 533–9)

The account of Troilus's anguished feelings is sharply poignant: the
sudden chill at his heart, the pallor, and the abrupt spurring of his
horse 'withouten word', so that no one shall see his pain, convey a
wounding experience in terms which strike directly home. Yet
however sensitive and moving, this is not writing which could
pass as colloquial. Its manner is not spoken but written, and that
fact helps to give the passage a gravity which makes us more
readily sympathise with Troilus in his desolation.

Critics are generally agreed that although written in rhyme
royal, *The Prioress' Tale* belongs to the final period and was
probably composed with Madam Eglantine in mind. Chaucer's
decision to use rhyme royal was perhaps influenced by the
Prioress's yearning for social distinction, and also by a need to set
the tale and its miracle at some distance from the matter-of-fact

level of existence which the Host personifies. It is a recital calculated to impress the Prioress's travelling companions by its piety and tender-heartedness, complementing the effect she has already created by her fastidiousness at table and the tears shed over dead mice. The pathos of her tale is its obvious courtly feature. The 'litel clergeon' whose love for the Virgin dominates his life appeals both to pietistic feeling and to the 'tendre herte' which the Prioress likes to display, especially since the boy appears to be a widow's only child. Instructed by his mother, he kneels in reverence before every statue of the Virgin which he passes on his way to school, where he is a somewhat overzealous pupil. Attracted by the singing of *Alma redemptoris mater*, although quite ignorant of its meaning, he edges closer to the senior class until he knows its opening stanza by heart, meanwhile neglecting his primer. He then begs an older friend to translate the anthem for him and to explain its religious significance:

> This preyde he him to construe and declare
> Ful often time upon his knowes bare.   (76–7)

His bare knees suggest how earnestly the boy pleads for understanding of a religious matter thought too advanced for a seven-year-old. Although his friend can tell him only that the anthem is addressed to the Virgin,

> Hire to salute, and eek hire for to preye
> To been oure help and socour whan we deye   (81–2)

that is enough to make him promise immediately to learn the whole work as soon as he can, no matter what trouble follows:

> 'Now certes, I wol do my diligence
> To konne it al er Christemasse be went.
> Though that I for my primer shal be shent,

And shal be beten thries in an houre,
I wol it konne Oure Lady to honoure!'   (87–91)

If there is a hint of comedy in the boy's undertaking, his willingness to risk punishment for the sake of honouring the Virgin subdues it. He will indeed suffer for his dedicated service. Learning the anthem day by day from his friend, he is soon able to sing it faultlessly, and makes it his custom to fill the streets with the Virgin's praise as he walks to and from school:

The swetnesse hath his herte perced so
Of Cristes mooder that, to hire to preye,
He kan nat stinte of singing by the weye.   (103–5)

In the words of the Prioress's proem, 'laude precious' is being rendered to the Mother of Christ through the mouth of a child, whose song bursts from him in an ecstasy of spiritual joy. But prompted by Satan and enraged by such homage to Mary within their ghetto, the Jews put an end to his carefree singing by cutting his throat. Increasingly perturbed by her son's failure to return home, after a sleepless night his mother begins a distracted search which eventually carries her into the ghetto. There her calls are answered by her son's voice, singing his anthem at the top of his voice from the foul pit where his murderers have flung him. Still singing, his body is carried to a nearby abbey and questioned by the abbot about its miraculous ability to continue its song of praise despite its savagely mutilated throat. The three stanzas of dialogue which follow constitute the high point of the poem's courtliness. Speaking with a grave and lyrical simplicity, the boy tells of his love for the Virgin which brought her to him in the last moments of his life, to place a small pearl upon his tongue with the bidding that he continue to sing her anthem. 'Wherfore I singe,' the martyred boy explains,

> 'and singe moot, certeyn,
> In honour of that blisful Maiden free,
> Til fro my tongue of taken is the greyn;
> And after that thus seyde she to me:
> "My litel child, now wol I fecche thee,
> Whan that the greyn is fro thy tonge ytake,
> Be nat agast, I wol thee nat forsake." '   (211–17)

The Virgin's speech, and its kindly assurance to the dying boy, round off the episode with a promise of maternal care and protection with which the Prioress might unconsciously associate herself. The little clergeon has lost his widowed mother, but has found a far more comprehensive figure of maternal love in the Virgin, whose nature is not so remote that the Prioress cannot partly identify herself with it. As a nun, she is vowed to chastity as complete as Mary's; and although not a mother in the literal sense, the woman described in *The General Prologue* certainly appears to have a strong maternal impulse. Kittredge went too far in seeing in her 'the poignant trait of thwarted motherhood',[1] but he was looking in the right direction. Small and helpless creatures hold an irresistible attraction for the Prioress, not simply because she longs for a child but because 'conscience' or courtly sensibility requires her to display tenderly affectionate feelings towards the young and defenceless, whether human or not. Chaucer's fondness for the maxim 'Pitee renneth soone in gentil herte'[2] indicates how a woman who wished to be regarded as coming from a noble family should fashion her behaviour. The passages of *The Prioress' Tale* which appeal directly to the softer emotions support Madam Eglantine's doubtful claim to gentle status.

---

[1] Chaucer and his Poetry, Harvard 1915, p. 178.

[2] 'Noble and generous natures are quickly moved by compassion.' The comment occurs in *The Knight's Tale*, I, 1761; *The Merchant's Tale*, IV, 1986; *The Squire's Tale*, V, 479; and *The Legend of Good Women*, F, 503.

But it is no courtly audience which is struck dumb by her story, and the oddly assorted company of pilgrims show that they too are susceptible to the deeper feelings which her tale evokes. These include religious awe; not an inappropriate response in a company bound for the shrine of another martyr at Canterbury, though one ignored in the Host's assumption that the journey will become tedious unless the pilgrims decide 'to talen and to pleye'[1] along the road. Whatever distance separated courtly sensibility from the rasping uncouthness of churls like the Miller and the Summoner, in the field of religious experience the differences were probably much less important. Medieval faith was supported by a great deal of superstition and credulity, neither of them confined to the lower classes. The suggestion that the Virgin might intervene in human affairs and miraculously enable a murdered boy to sing despite his severed throat did not then seem fanciful, as it must to us. The pilgrimages which took medieval folk across Europe in their thousands despite the difficulties of travelling were no doubt a sincere expression of faith; but a faith inextricably mixed with childish fears and expectations closer to folklore and occult practices than to religious truth. Chaucer's pilgrims are silenced by the Prioress's story not so much because they are pious at heart as because its account of a miracle engages the deeply superstitious feelings that seem to have dominated medieval outlook on religion for the people.

Finally, however, the force of *The Prioress' Tale* is explained neither by its courtliness nor by its religious appeal, but by the controlled power of its narrative. In his earlier poems, Chaucer's courtly manner was marked by a leisured pace which allowed time for detailed description and passages of unhurried dialogue. The brevity of *The Prioress' Tale* must be intentional, and a consequence of its terseness and economy. Like the Clerk whose

---

[1] 'To tell stories and to amuse themselves', *The General Prologue*, 772.

character is sketched in *The General Prologue*, Chaucer seems to have rejected prolixity in favour of a pithy conciseness which carries the reader through his story with a minimum of digressions and literary flourishes. Rhetoric is largely confined to the opening address to the Virgin, a consciously artificial piece of writing whose formality lasts only until the Prioress embarks on her tale. Just seven lines of colloquially simple description set the scene:

> Ther was in Asie, in a greet citee,
> Amonges Cristene folk, a Jewerie,
> Sustened by a lord of that contree
> For foule usure and lucre of vileynie,
> Hateful to Crist and to his compaignie;
> And thurgh the strete men mighte ride or wende,
> For it was free and open at either ende.   (36–42)

A Christian city in a distant country, containing a ghetto easy of access, where the wicked practice of usury was tolerated: the setting is rapidly put together, with strong hints of the tension between Christian virtue and the evil represented by 'foule usure and lucre of vileynie', a phrase heavy with disgust and scorn. The opening words of the next stanza introduce the 'litel scole' where the widow's son studies his primer. In fewer than eight lines the broad field of view is narrowed and focused upon the particular locality where the action of the tale is to occur.

The compression of Chaucer's writing is more easily recognised in the obviously dramatic passages of the story. At line 106, Satan puts it into the Jews' mind that the boy's singing is an insult to their religion. This evil insinuation drops into the narrative as an isolated stanza, and motivates the crime described only a dozen or so lines later in a terse, impersonal report:

> An homicide therto han they hired,
> That in an aleye hadde a privee place;
> And as the child gan forby for to pacc,
> This cursed Jew him hente, and heeld him faste,
> And kitte his throte, and in a pit him caste.   (115–19)

Such economy reminds us of Chaucer's approving remark about the Clerk: 'Noght o word spak he moore than was neede.' Only the epithet 'cursed' could be omitted without damaging the sense, for the narrative does not compromise its starkness by adding gruesome details. The speed of the account matches the horrible suddenness of the boy's death, and its lack of emotion suggests the unfeeling brutality of the crime. Much the same terseness accompanies the description of the provost's actions in arresting the murderers and sentencing them to death. He comes into the story at line 164, and after an intervening stanza dealing with the procession to the abbey he figures centrally in the next seven lines before vanishing from the poem:

> With torment and with shameful deeth echon
> This provost dooth thise Jewes for to sterve
> That of this mordre wiste, and that anon.
> He nolde no swich cursednesse observe.
> 'Yvele shal have that yvele wol deserve';
> Therfore with wilde hors he dide hem drawe,
> And after that he heng hem by the lawe.   (176–82)

The contained energy of the writing gives force to the provost's angry condemnation of the murder, in a proverbial saying which might have been taken as a model of succinctness. The generally worn phrase 'and that anon' contributes positively to the stanza because its promise of immediacy matches the speed and decisiveness of the passage: things are indeed happening rapidly as the matter is summarily dealt with and abruptly put aside.

These examples of Chaucer's compressed narrative style happen to deal with material issues and fact, while the general concern of the tale is religious, and its main event a miracle. Such a narrative manner, we might suppose, would be unsympathetic to this central interest; but in fact the bare, laconic style helps to make the miraculous credible, rather than the opposite. When the murdered boy answers the abbot's questions about his ability to sing despite a fearful wound to the throat, he speaks with a simple directness which treats the miracle as a matter of course:

> 'My throte is kut unto my nekke boon,'
> Seyde this child, 'and, as by wey of kinde,
> I sholde have died, ye, longe time agon.
> But Jesu Crist, as ye in bookes finde,
> Wil that his glories laste and be in minde,
> And for the worship of his Mooder deere
> Yet may I singe *O Alma* loude and cleere.' (197–203)

By describing his wound and its normal consequences so calmly, the boy makes the miraculous seem a part of everyday affairs: what has happened conforms with faith and does not tax human understanding. He speaks to the abbot not as a child to an adult but as his spiritual equal, and the unexpected phrase 'as ye in bookes finde' – which seems to imply a knowledge of theology much wider than the boy could have acquired at school – indicates quite plainly why the miracle should have happened. The level tone of the boy's statement requires us to accept his explanation in the same undisturbed spirit.

Chaucer's handling of his narrative as it shifts from the mundane to the miraculous is an unobtrusive sign of his craftsmanship. Throughout the tale the worlds of spirit and mundane reality repeatedly rub against one another, most obviously in the boy's devoted love of the Virgin and the fiendish malice which his pure-hearted singing arouses. The opening stanza of the tale, we have seen, establishes a moral tension between 'Cristene folk' and a force of malevolent evil 'hateful to Crist': the ghetto represents a malignant enclave within a Christian society, yet 'free and open at either ende'. As the story develops, telling how the boy makes his daily journey through the ghetto, singing his anthem, it involves another moral dichotomy; now between *O Alma* with its theme of divine redemption and the quarter of dark alleys and hidden entrances where a murderer lurks. The constrast is stated more emphatically when the murdered boy's body is tumbled into a common privy, and although mutilated and defiled continues to sing its praises of the Virgin. As if the murder were not outrageous enough, the Prioress amplifies her first account of the crime to reveal how shamefully the victim's body is treated:

> I seye that in a wardrobe they him threwe,
> Where as thise Jewes purgen hire entraille.   (120–1)

Coming from the fastidious Prioress, the disclosure is doubly shocking in its frankness; but the attempt to degrade the boy is as unsuccessful as the wish to silence him. When his mother goes through the ghetto crying his name, he answers by resuming his anthem in a voice stronger than his own:

> Ther he with throte ykorven lay upright,
> He *Alma redemptoris* gan to singe
> So loude that al the place gan to ringe.   (159–61)

Whether 'the place' is the privy into which he has been thrown or its evil surroundings, his physical environment is made to reverberate as a pure spiritual force asserts itself over material squalor. The child whom the Prioress calls 'this gemme of chastite, this emeraude' shines from his filthy setting with still greater brilliance, and innocence triumphs over the evil of a repulsively corrupted world.

Modern readers of the poem are likely to be troubled by the fact that this evil is embodied in a Jewish community, whose ghetto shelters every kind of detestable wickedness. The belief that the Jews were a cursed race, deserving to be persecuted for practices 'hateful to Christ', seems astonishing in the Prioress, who is otherwise anxious to display tender and compassionate feelings; and it raises the question whether she or Chaucer is responsible for the antisemitism of the tale. To take the second view is certainly possible, for Chaucer too was exposed to the savage prejudices of his age, but it carries the implication that he did not recognise how inhuman the persecution was. It makes for a less uncomfortable reading of the story to assume that the Prioress rather than the poet suffers from moral myopia. That, of course, is no adequate reason for regarding Chaucer as above racial and religious prejudice, though his stinging attack on the Friar in *The General Prologue* shows a contempt for those who make their faith justify cruelty and neglect. But it would be characteristic of Chaucer's irony to reveal a streak of inhumanity beneath the Prioress's sentimental regard for pets, and a fierce racial hatred coexisting with tearful softness. His satire thrived on such contradictions.

But perhaps a modern reader attaches too much significance to the antisemitic aspects of *The Prioress' Tale*, forgetting that fear and hatred were the common reaction to whatever lay beyond the confines of the medieval world. For Chaucer himself, who had travelled in France and Italy, those confines were broader than for most of his fellow countrymen, yet even he writes about countries outside Christendom as though they were merely savage and fearful. No doubt literary tradition encouraged a view that persisted at least until the date of Shakespeare's *Othello*, that heathendom was peopled by monstrous beings made more horrible by their idolatry; but medieval imagination was darkened by visions of nightmarish figures and situations which found their fullest expression in pictures of Hell and the torments of the

damned. Although this subject seems not to have troubled
Chaucer as it did many of his contemporaries, grotesque and
repulsive creatures live in the background of his awareness. The
three pilgrims described at the end of *The General Prologue*
– Reeve, Summoner and Pardoner – are a manifestation of
spiritual ugliness better suited to a medieval Hell's mouth than to
an April morning. The devilish Jews of *The Prioress' Tale* may be
derived from the same imaginative source. Like the leprous
Summoner and the implacably hostile Reeve, they seem to give
shape to the poet's sense of a destructively evil force at large in the
world of his belief. In *The Canterbury Tales* this force is successfully
challenged by the comic purpose which sustains the whole work;
but other medieval poets and painters appear less certain than
Chaucer that evil could be contained by an impulse of creative
vitality.

But the antisemitic elements of *The Prioress' Tale* cannot be
dismissed simply as an expression of unacknowledged fears and
terrors preying upon the medieval mind. For nearly three
centuries before the writing of *The Canterbury Tales* the Jews in
Europe had been repeatedly subjected to persecution of a kind
not seen again until Hitler's attempt to eliminate the so-called
Jewish problem. Although Chaucer lived in an England from
which the Jews had been expelled, the history of this persecution
lingered as part of the atmosphere in which he lived and formed
opinions. Until the later part of the eleventh century, European
Jews seem generally to have been well treated, earning adequate
livelihoods and maintaining good relations with their Christian
neighbours, despite local customs which revealed an underlying
resentment of their religious attitude. One historian mentions a
yearly tradition during Easter week in the French town of Beziers
of pelting the Jews with mud and stones, in retribution for the
sufferings of Christ. In Toulouse a similar custom gave the local
count the right to slap the face of the Jewish leader on Good

Friday.[1] Such spiteful observances became increasingly common in consequence of the First Crusade, launched by Pope Urban in 1095. By promoting the idea that there were enemies of Christ nearer home than Jerusalem, the crusaders encouraged riots and massacres in Germany and Bohemia in which thousands of Jews perished. Nearly half a century later, when the Second Crusade was being organised, a similar argument was advanced: it was pointless to carry war against the Saracens in a distant country when so many blasphemers were living comfortably in Europe. Where previously it had been possible for Jews to live unmolested in Christian communities, the Crusades sharpened religious hatred to the point where the Jews were popularly regarded as an accursed race, rightly suffering for their rejection of Christ. To persecute them was almost a duty, as Innocent III indicated in a letter summarising his policy: 'The Jews, like the fratricide Cain, are doomed to wander about the earth as fugitives and vagabonds, and their faces must be covered in shame. They are under no circumstances to be protected by Christian princes, but on the contrary to be condemned to serfdom.' To make persecution easier, Innocent decreed in 1251 that all Jews should wear a badge on their clothing distinguishing them from Christians.

With antisemitism thus recommended by the Pope, the thirteenth century was understandably a period of increasing danger and grinding hardship for the Jews, with popular hostility expressing itself in slanderous allegations and tales. The blood of Christian children was said to be used in Jewish religious rites, and stories of child murder were revived from earlier times to inflame opinion against the Jewish communities. Fifteen years after Innocent's decree, Henry III forced the English Jews to give up one-third of their property in taxes. In 1264, riots in London during Easter week resulted in the deaths of some 1500 Jews; and

---

[1] Sachar, *A History of the Jews*, 5th edn, New York, 1968, p. 186.

in 1275, Edward I forbade the practice of usury, which denied the Jews one of the few means of livelihood left open to them. Finally, in 1290 the king ordered a general expulsion of Jews from England, in an edict which was not annulled until the middle of the seventeenth century, when Cromwell permitted a limited return. Thus during Chaucer's lifetime the Jews were strangers to the country, and the antisemitism of *The Prioress' Tale* cannot be seen as reflecting the poet's private experience but as an inherited prejudice which had passed into popular legend. Chaucer may have encountered Jews during his continental missions, but the tradition behind medieval tales of murdered boys was not dependent upon the realities of Jewish behaviour. Religious prejudice, misrepresentation and hatred of an alien people had built up a caricature of blasphemous evil, greed and brutality which served much the same purpose in literature as the ogres and demons of folklore. It looks as though the Jews were being used to objectify some of the terrors which haunted the consciousness of a superstition-ridden age.

The savage persecution of the Jews in central Europe during the years of the Black Death (1348–1349) may support this suggestion. Although the plague was widely attributed to God's wrath against a sinful mankind, a belief sprang up that the disease had its source in wells poisoned by the Jews. In September 1348 a group of Swiss Jews was seized for such a crime, and put to torture to extract a detailed confession of guilt. With this contrived evidence to justify persecution,

> in Basle all the Jews were penned up in wooden buildings and burnt alive . . . In November 1348 the Jews were burnt at Solothurn, Zofingen and Stuttgart; in December at Landsberg, Burren, Memmingen, Lindau; in January, Freiburg, Ulm and

Speyer. At Speyer the bodies of the murdered were piled in
great wine-casks and sent floating down the Rhine.[1]

In England the expulsion of the Jews nearly sixty years earlier
removed the obvious target of such terrified mob hysteria, but the
many analogues of *The Prioress' Tale* show that popular legend was
keeping hatred of the Jews alive despite their long absence from
the country. The miracle plays, graphically depicting Christ's
buffeting, scourging and crucifixion at the hands of Jewish
torturers – though Christ's suffering must have been inflicted by
Roman soldiers – helped to fix the idea of sadistic cruelty and
monstrous evil in the popular mind as characterising the Jew. The
fact that Chaucer adopted this view in *The Prioress' Tale* should not
be taken as a sign of inhumanity or thoughtlessness. The tale of
the murdered boy assigned to the Prioress depended upon hatred
of the Christian faith for its motivation of the crime. That was the
story known in one version or another to Chaucer's wider
audience, and it was not his purpose to attack the racial prejudice
inseparable from the tale. His task was to refashion a popular
legend so that in its retelling it became something more than a
familiar story and was transformed into an enduring work of art.

---

[1] Ziegler, *The Black Death*, London 1969, pp. 104–5.

Note on the text

The text which follows is based upon that of F. N. Robinson (*The Complete Works of Geoffrey Chaucer*, 2nd ed., 1957). The punctuation has been revised, with special reference to the exclamation marks. Spelling has been partly rationalised, by substituting *i* for *y* wherever the change does not affect the semantic value of the word. Thus *smylying* becomes 'smiling', and *nyghtyngale* 'nightingale', but *wyn* (wine), *lyk* (like), and *fyr* (fire) are allowed to stand.

Note on pronunciation

These equivalences are intended to offer only a rough guide.

Short vowels

    ă represents the sound now written *u*, as in 'cut'
    ĕ as in modern 'set'
    ĭ as in modern 'is'
    ŏ as in modern 'top'
    ŭ as in modern 'put' (not as in 'cut ')
    final -*e* represents the neutral vowel sound in '*a*bout' or 'atten*ti*on'. It is silent when the next word in the line begins with a vowel or an *h*.

Long vowels

    ā as in modern 'car' (not as in 'name')
    ē (open—i.e. where the equivalent modern word is spelt with *ea*) as in modern 'there'
    ē (close—i.e. where the equivalent modern word is spelt with *ee* or *e*) represents the sound now written *a* as in 'take'
    ī as in modern 'machine' (not as in 'like')

$\bar{o}$ (open—i.e. where the equivalent modern vowel is pronounced as in 'brother', 'mood' or 'good') represents the sound now written *aw* as in 'fawn'

$\bar{o}$ (close—i.e. where the equivalent modern vowel is pronounced as in 'road') as in modem 'note'

$\bar{u}$ as in French *tu* or German *Tür*

Diphthongs

ai and *ei* both roughly represent the sound now written *i* or *y* as in 'die' or 'dye'

au and *aw* both represent the sound now written *ow* or *ou* as in 'now' or 'pounce'

ou and *ow* have two pronunciations: as in *through* where the equivalent modern vowel is pronounced as in 'through' or 'mouse'; and as in *pounce* where the equivalent modern vowel is pronounced as in 'known' or 'thought'

Writing of vowels and diphthongs

A long vowel is often indicated by doubling, as in *roote* or *eek*. The $\breve{u}$ sound is sometimes represented by an *o* as in *young*. The *au* sound is sometimes represented by an *a*, especially before *m* or *n*, as in *cha(u)mbre* or *cha(u)nce*.

Consonants

Largely as in modern English, except that many consonants now silent were still pronounced. *Gh* was pronounced as in Scottish 'loch', and both consonants should be pronounced in such groups as the following: '*gn*acchen', '*kn*ave', 'wor*d*', 'fol*k*', '*wr*ong'.

The Portrait of the Prioress

(From *The General Prologue*, lines 118–62)

Ther was also a Nonne, a PRIORESSE,
That of hir smiling was ful simple and coy;
Hire gretteste ooth was but by Seinte Loy;
And she was cleped madame Eglentine.
Ful weel she soong the service divine,
Enturned in hir nose ful semely,
And Frenssh she spak ful faire and fetisly,
After the scole of Stratford atte Bowe,
For Frenssh of Paris was to hire unknowe.
At mete wel ytaught was she with alle:
She leet no morsel from hir lippes falle,
Ne wette hir fingres in hir sauce depe;
Wel koude she carie a morsel and wel kepe
That no drope ne fille upon hire brest.
In curteisie was set ful muchel hir lest.
Hir over-lippe wiped she so clene
That in hir coppe ther was no ferthing sene
Of grece, when she dronken hadde hir draughte.
Ful semely after hir mete she raughte.
And sikerly she was of greet desport,
And ful plesaunt, and amiable of port,
And peyned hire to countrefete cheere
Of court, and to been estatlich of manere,
And to ben holden digne of reverence.
But, for to speken of hire conscience,
She was so charitable and so pitous
She wolde wepe, if that she saugh a mous
Kaught in a trappe, if it were deed or bledde.
Of smale houndes hadde she that she fedde

With rosted flessh, or milk and wastel-breed.
But soore wepte she if oon of hem were deed,
Or if men smoot it with a yerde smerte;
And al was conscience and tendre herte.
Ful semely hir wimpul pinched was,
Hir nose tretis, hir eyen greye as glas,
Hir mouth ful smal, and therto softe and reed;
But sikerly she hadde a fair forheed;
It was almoost a spanne brood, I trowe;
For, hardily, she was not undergrowe.
Ful fetis was hir cloke, as I was war.
Of smal coral aboute hire arm she bar
A peire of bedes, gauded al with grene,
And theron heng a brooch of gold ful sheene,
On which ther was first write a crowned A,
And after *Amor vincit omnia.*

The Prioress' Prologue

'O Lord, oure Lord, thy name how merveillous
Is in this large world ysprad,' quod she;
'For noght oonly thy laude precious
Parfourned is by men of dignitee,
But by the mouth of children thy bountee
Parfourned is, for on the brest soukinge
Somtime shewen they thyn heryinge.

Wherfore in laude, as I best kan or may,
Of thee and of the white lilye flour
Which that the bar, and is a maide alway,   10
To telle a storie I wol do my labour;
Nat that I may encressen hir honour,
For she hirself is honour and the roote
Of bountee, next hir Sone, and soules boote.

O mooder Maide! o maide Mooder free!
O bussh unbrent, brenninge in Moyses sighte,
That ravishedest doun fro the Deitee,
Thurgh thyn humblesse, the Goost that in
     th'alighte,
Of whos vertu, whan he thyn herte lighte,
Conceived was the Fadres sapience,   20
Help me to telle it in thy reverence!

Lady, thy bountee, thy magnificence,
Thy vertu, and thy grete humilitee,
There may no tonge expresse in no science;
For somtime, Lady, er men praye to thee,
Thou goost biforn of thy beningnitee,
And getest us the light, of thy preyere,

To gyden us unto thy Sone so deere.

My konning is so wayk, o blisful Queene,
For to declare thy grete worthinesse   30
That I ne may the weighte nat susteene;
But as a child of twelf month oold, or lesse,
That kan unnethes any word expresse,
Right so fare I, and therefore I yow preye,
Gydeth my song that I shal of yow seye.'

The Prioress' Tale

Ther was in Asie, in a greet citee,
Amonges Cristene folk, a Jewerie,
Sustened by a lord of that contree
For foule usure and lucre of vileinie,
Hateful to Crist and to his compaignie;   40
And thurgh the strete men mighte ride or
        wende,
For it was free and open at either ende.

A litel scole of Cristen folk ther stood
Doun at the ferther ende, in which ther were
Children an heep, ycomen of Cristen blood,
That lerned in that scole yeer by yere
Swich manere doctrine as men used there,
This is to seyn, to singen and to rede,
As smale children doon in hire childhede.

Among thise children was a widwes sone,   50
A litel clergeon, seven yeer of age,
That day by day to scole was his wone,
And eek also, where as he saugh th'image
Of Cristes mooder, hadde he in usage,
As him was taught, to knele adoun and seye
His *Ave Marie*, as he goth by the weye.

Thus hath this widwe hir litel sone ytaught
Oure blisful Lady, Cristes mooder deere,
To worshipe ay, and he forgat it naught,
For sely child wol alday soone leere.   60
But ay, whan I remembre on this mateere,
Seint Nicholas stant evere in my presence,

For he so yong to Crist dide reverence.

This litel child, his litel book lerninge,
As he sat in the scole at his primer,
He *Alma redemptoris* herde singe,
As children lerned hire antiphoner;
And as he dorste, he drough him ner and ner
And herkened ay the wordes and the noote,
Til he the firste vers koude al by rote.   70

Noght wiste he what this Latin was to seye,
For he so yong and tendre was of age.
But on a day his felawe gan he preye
T'expounden him this song in his langage,
Or telle him why this song was in usage;
This preyde he him to construe and declare
Ful often time upon his knowes bare.

His felawe, which that elder was than he,
Answerde him thus: 'This song, I have herd
                        seye,
Was maked of our blisful Lady free,   80
Hire to salue, and eek hire for to preye
To been oure help and socour whan we deye.
I kan namoore expounde in this mateere;
I lerne song, I kan but smal grammeere.'

'And is this song maked in reverence
Of Cristes mooder?' seide this innocent.
'Now, certes, I wol do my diligence
To konne it al er Cristemasse be went.
Though that I for my primer shal be shent,
And shal be beten thries in an houre,   90
I wol it konne Oure Lady for to honoure !'

His felawe taughte him homward prively,
Fro day to day, til he koude it by rote,
And thanne he song it wel and boldely,
Fro word to word, acordinge with the note.
Twies a day it passed thurgh his throte,
To scoleward and homward whan he wente;
On Cristes mooder set was his entente.

As I have seyd, thurghout the Juerie,
This litel child, as he cam to and fro,   100
Ful murily than wolde he singe and crie
O Alma redemptoris everemo.
The swetnesse hath his herte perced so
Of Cristes moder that, to hire to preye,
He kan nat stinte of singing by the weye.

Oure firste foo, the serpent Sathanas,
That hath in Jues herte his waspes nest,
Up swal, and seide, 'O Hebraik peple, allas!
Is this to yow a thing that is honest,
That swich a boy shal walken as him lest   110
In youre despit, and singe of swich sentence,
Which is again youre lawes reverence?'

Fro thennes forth the Jues han conspired
This innocent out of this world to chace.
An homicide therto han they hired,
That in an aleye hadde a privee place;
And as the child gan forby for to pace,
This cursed Jew him hente, and heeld him
        faste,
And kitte his throte, and in a pit him caste.

I seye that in a wardrobe they him threwe   120
Where as thise Jewes purgen hire entraille.
O cursed folk of Herodes al newe,
What may youre yvel entente yow availle?
Mordre wol out, certein, it wol nat faille,
And namely ther th'onour of God shal sprede;
The blood out crieth on youre cursed dede.

O martir, sowded to virginitee,
Now maistow singen, folwinge evere in oon
The white Lamb celestial – quod she –
Of which the grete evaungelist, Seint John,   130
In Pathmos wroot, which seith that they that
        goon
Biforn this Lamb, and singe a song al newe,
That nevere, flesshly, wommen they ne
    knewe.

This poure widwe awaiteth al that night
After hir litel child, but he cam noght;
For which, as soone as it was dayes light,
With face pale of drede and bisy thoght,
She hath at scole and elleswhere him soght,
Til finally she gan so fer espie
That he last seyn was in the Juerie.   140

With moodres pitee in hir brest enclosed,
She gooth, as she were half out of hir minde,
To every place where she hath supposed
By liklihede hir litel child to finde;
And evere on Cristes mooder meeke and kinde
She cride, and atte laste thus she wroghte :
Among the cursed Jues she him soghte.

She frayneth and she preyeth pitously
To every Jew that dwelte in thilke place,
To telle hire if hir child went oght forby.   150
They seide 'nay'; but Jhesu, of his grace,
Yaf in hir thoght, inwith a litel space,
That in that place after hir sone she cride,
Where he was casten in a pit biside.

O grete God, that parfournest thy laude
By mouth of innocentz, lo, heere thy might!
This gemme of chastite, this emeraude,
And eek of martirdom the ruby bright,
Ther he with throte ykorven lay upright,
He *Alma redemptoris* gan to singe   160
So loude that al the place gan to ringe.

The Cristene folk that thurgh the strete
          wente
In coomen for to wondre upon this thing,
And hastily they for the provost sente;
He cam anon withouten tarying,
And herieth Crist that is of hevene king,
And eek his mooder, honour of mankinde,
And after that the Jewes leet he binde.

This child with pitous lamentacioun
Up taken was, singinge his song alway,   170
And with honour of greet processioun
They carien him unto the nexte abbay.
His mooder swowninge by the beere lay;
Unnethe mighte the peple that was theere
This newe Rachel bringe fro his beere.

With torment and with shameful deeth
     echon
This provost dooth thise Jewes for to sterve
That of this mordre wiste, and that anon.
He nolde no swich cursednesse observe.
'Yvele shal have that yvele wol deserve';   180
Therefore with wilde hors he dide hem drawe,
And after that he heng hem by the lawe.

   Upon this beere ay lith this innocent
Biforn the chief auter, whil masse laste;
And after that, the abbot with his covent
Han sped hem for to burien him ful faste;
And whan they hooly water on him caste,
Yet spak this child, whan spreynd was hooly
     water,
And song O Alma redemptoris mater!

   This abbot, which that was an hooly man,   190
As monkes been – or elles oghte be –
This yonge child to conjure he bigan,
And seide, 'O deere child, I halse thee,
In vertu of the hooly Trinitee,
Tel me what is thy cause for to singe,
Sith that thy throte is kut to my seminge?'

   'My throte is kut unto my nekke boon,'
Seide this child, 'and, as by wey of kinde,
I sholde have died, ye, longe time agon.
But Jesus Crist, as ye in bookes finde,   200
Wil that his glorie laste and be in minde,
And for the worship of his Mooder deere
Yet may I sing O Alma loude and cleere.

'This welle of mercy, Cristes mooder
    sweete,
I loved alwey, as after my konninge;
And whan that I my lyf sholde forlete,
To me she cam, and bad me for to singe
This anthem verraily in my deyinge,
As ye han herd, and whan that I hadde songe,
Me thoughte she leide a greyn upon my tonge.   210

'Wherefore I singe, and singe moot certeyn,
In honour of that blisful Maiden free,
Til fro my tonge of taken is the greyn;
And after that thus seide she to me :
"My litel child, now wol I fecche thee,
Whan that the greyn is fro thy tonge ytake.
Be nat agast, I wol thee nat forsake." '

This hooly monk, this abbot, him meene I,
His tonge out caughte, and took awey the
    greyn,
And he yaf up the goost ful softely.   220
And whan this abbot hadde this wonder seyn,
His salte teeris trikled doun as reyn,
And gruf he fil al plat upon the grounde,
And stille he lay as he had ben ybounde.

The covent eek lay on the pavement
Wepinge, and herying Cristes mooder deere,
And after that they rise, and forth been went,
And tooken awey this martir from his beere;
And in a tombe of marbul stones cleere
Enclosen they his litel body sweete.   230
Ther he is now, God leve us for to meete!

O yonge Hugh of Lincoln, slain also
With cursed Jewes, as it is notable,
For it is but a litel while ago,
Preye eek for us, we sinful folk unstable,
That, of his mercy, God so merciable
On us his grete mercy multiplie,
For reverence of his mooder Marie.
                    Amen.

Heere is ended the Prioresses Tale.

Notes

The Prioress' Prologue

The Prioress' Prologue, more properly described as a proem, consists of an address to the Virgin Mary and an appeal for her help in telling the legend that follows. Similar invocations occur in Chaucer's *Parlement of Foules* (113–19), where the dreamer asks Venus to give him 'might to ryme', and at the great opening of Book III of *Troilus and Criseyde*, also addressed to Venus. Like her companion the Second Nun, the Prioress appropriately directs her praises to a central figure of the Christian faith instead of to a pagan goddess. By giving her prologue a literary form respected by medieval poets and rhetoricians – that of an invocation followed by an appeal – she lends dignity to this opening address.

The substance of the first stanza, briefly restated in lines 155–6, is taken from the opening verses of Psalm 8: 'O Lord our Lord, how excellent is thy name in all the earth! who hast set thy glory above the heavens. Out of the mouths of babes and sucklings hast thou ordained strength, because of thine enemies, that thou mightest still the enemy and the avenger.'

4. *men of dignitee* 'people of high rank and importance'.

7. *shewen they thyn heryinge* 'utter thy praises'.

8. *as I best kan* or *may* 'to the best of my knowledge and ability'. Medieval *kan* from *konnen* is a strong verb, not an auxiliary, meaning 'know how to do'. See line 84 for a clear example of this sense.

9. *the white lilye flour* symbolising the Virgin Mary.

10. *which that the bar* 'who bore thee'.

11. *do my labour* 'make my best effort'.

14. *next hir Sone* 'second only to Christ' in goodness.

16. *O bussh unbrent* see Exodus 3:2–4 for the story behind this allusion. Chaucer refers to this alternative symbol of the Virgin Mary in one of his earliest poems, *An ABC* (89–91).

Moises, that saugh the bushe with flawmes rede
Brenninge, of which ther never a stikke brende,
Was signe of thyn unwemmed maidenhede.
(*unwemmed* = unspotted)

17–18. *That ravishedest doun . . . in th'alighte* 'whose lowliness attracted the Holy Spirit so irresistibly that it descended from God and took possession of you.'

19–20. *Of whos vertu . . . Fadres sapience* 'by whose power, illuminating your soul, God's wisdom was engendered' in Mary. The heart was regarded as the source of man's deepest thoughts and feelings, and so associated with the soul or spirit. The passage is reminiscent of Chaucer's reference to the April showers 'of which vertu engendred is the flour' in *The General Prologue*, 1–4.

21. *in thy reverence* 'with great veneration of you'.

24. *no tonge expresse in no science* The double negative is emphatic: 'no form of speech, however learned, can possibly describe'.

26. *of thy beningnitee* 'through your graciousness'. The idea that the Virgin Mary sometimes answers men's needs before they pray for them comes from Dante's *Paradiso* xxxiii, 16 in a stanza referring to Mary's *benignita* and *magnificenza*.

27. *of thy preyere* 'by your intercession'. See note on line 235.

31. *ne may the weighte nat susteene* Another emphatic negative construction: 'I am totally unable to carry out such a task'. Her modesty is a familiar Chaucerian attitude: see *The Knight's Tale*, I, 887; *The Franklin's Prologue*, V, 718–19; *The Monk's Prologue*, VII, 1990; *The Second Nun's Tale*, VIII, 78–80; and *The Parson's Prologue*, V 55–7 [in Robinson's edition].

32. *as a child of twelf month oold* The Prioress compares herself to an infant such as she has described in lines 5–7 above, which praises God though unable to speak. The parallel implies that she has not only the helplessness of a child but the same innocence and sincerity, and that these qualities will characterise her story.

35. *gydeth* the polite imperative form, 'guide ye'.

36. *Asie* Asia Minor is intended. Christendom did not extend beyond the western fringes of the Asian continent, which was largely unknown to Europeans at this time. See note on line 131.

37. *a Jewrie* a ghetto inside which Jews were obliged to live as a separate community, despised by Christian society.

39. *For foule usure and lucre of vileinie* 'for wicked usury and filthy lucre'. The Medieval Church forbade usury, charging interest on monetary loans. Jews, however, were not affected by this prohibition, and partly for this reason they assumed the role of money-lenders in European society. Robinson observes that the Jewish colony in medieval Norwich enjoyed the special protection of the king; a realistic measure, since however repugnant to the Church, usury was an unavoidable part of economic life. But the common prejudices against usury as a practice 'hateful to Crist' increased the general antagonism felt towards the Jews as enemies of Christendom.

41–2. The ghetto was not a closed area but part of a thoroughfare.

43. *a litel scole* Earlier commentators supposed that a choir school was meant. But the large number of pupils (l. 45) and the suggestion that some of them were taught Latin (l. 84) make it seem more likely that Chaucer had an ordinary school in mind.

44. *Doun at the ferther ende* beyond the ghetto, which stood between the school and the town centre.

45. *children an heep* 'a great number of children'. The article *an* suggests that *heep* was not aspirated. Compare *an homicide*, line 115. *of Cristen blood* 'of Christian parents'.

47. *Swich manere doctrine as men used there* 'the kind of instruction which was provided there'. The term *men* is impersonal, like *Man* in German and *on* in French.

48. *to singen and to rede* 'The learning of anthems was part of the regular instruction in medieval English schools'– Robinson, p. 735.

51. *clergeon* A small 'clerk' or literate person; a schoolboy and not specifically a chorister.

52. *That day by day to scole was his wone* 'whose daily habit was (to go) to school'.

53. *eek also* 'in addition'.

53–4. *th'image of Cristes mooder* During the twelfth century a cult of the Virgin Mary spread across Europe, encouraging the production of such figures and statues.

54. *hadde he in usage* 'it was his habit'.

55. *him* the dative case, 'to him'.

56. *Ave Marie* 'Ave Maria', a short hymn of praise addressed to the Virgin.

60. *sely child wol alday soone leere* 'a good child is always quick to learn': a proverbial expression, generally in the shorter form, 'sely child is sone ylered',

62. *stant evere in my presence* 'always comes into my mind'. St Nicholas is reputed, as a child at the breast, to have fasted on Wednesdays and Fridays by taking only one feed.

65. *at his primer* the 'litel book' of the previous line, by which he is learning to read.

66. *Alma redemptoris* the opening words of the anthem, 'Alma redemptoris mater' (bounteous mother of redemption), sung in church between Advent and Candlemas – that is, over the Christmas season. The association helps to suggest that the 'litel clergeon' is linked with the innocents slaughtered by Herod soon after Christ's birth.

67. *hire antiphoner* 'their antiphoners' or anthem books. Antiphons are anthems or versicles sung by half the choir alternately responding to the other. These schoolchildren are at a more advanced stage of learning than the 'litel clergeon'.

68. *he drough him* 'he drew himself', edging as close as possible to the other class in another part of the same room.

70. *koude al by rote* 'knew it perfectly by heart'.

71. *was to seye* 'meant'.

73. *on a day* 'one day'.

gan he preye 'he begged' or besought. The verb *gan* is usually auxiliary, meaning 'did', as here. Occasionally Chaucer uses it in the sense 'began', as in line 160.

74. *in his langage* 'in his own tongue'.

75. *why this song was in usage* 'what was the purpose of this anthem'.

77. *upon his knowes bare* The picture of the little boy earnestly kneeling in his anxiety to have the anthem explained suggests his piety and reverence even before he knows that *Alma redemptoris* is addressed to the Virgin Mary.

78. *which that* 'who'.

80. *maked of* 'composed about' or for.

81. *eek hire for to preye* 'also as a means of imploring her'.

82. *oure help and sucour whan we deye* as indeed Mary will be to the 'litel clergeon', though much sooner than he could expect.

84. *I lerne song, I kan but smal grammeere* The friend is instructed in singing anthems but knows too little Latin to understand their meaning. The 'litel clergeon' too will sing *Alma redemptoris* without understanding more than the general sense of its being addressed to Mary, whom he venerates. Comprehension of the Latin words is not important; what matters is the attitude of sincere faith.

86. *this innocent* This expression, repeated in lines 114 and 183, again hints at a connection with the children murdered by Herod.

87. *I wol do my diligence* 'I will do my utmost', like the Prioress in telling the story.

88. *er Cristemasse be went* 'before Christmas is past'. The Prioress does not indicate what length of time this represents. The reference to Christmas might have been suggested by Chaucer's awareness of the slaughtered innocents in the background of the tale.

89. *Though that I for my primer shal be shent* 'though I should be punished for neglecting my primer'.

90. *beten thries in an houre* An unconsciously ironic remark. What faces the boy in consequence of neglecting his primer in favour of *Alma redemptoris* is violent death and martyrdom.

91. *for to honoure* 'in order to reverence'.

92. *prively* 'in private', as the boys went home together.

93. *Fro day to day* 'day by day'.

95. *Fro word to word* 'word by word'.

98. *On Cristes mooder set was his entente* 'his whole mind and purpose was concentrated on the mother of Christ'.

99. *thurghout the Juerie* 'from end to end of the Jewish quarter'.

104. *to hire to preye* 'in order to pray to her'.

105. *He han nat stinte of singing by the weye* 'he cannot stop singing along the road'.

106. *Oure firste foo* 'man's first enemy', who procured the fall in the guise of a serpent.

107. *his waspes nest* The idea of a serpent who lives in a wasps' nest is illogical, but the two images support a common notion of painful stinging and venom. The alliteration of 'waspes nest' creates an uncomfortable impression of hissing malice.

109. *Is this to yow a thing that is honest?* 'Does it seem right and proper to you?'

110. *as him lest* 'as it pleases him'.

111. *of swich sentence* 'of such a matter', meaning part of Christian faith.

112. *again youre lawes reverence* 'disrespectful to Jewish law'. Some medieval manuscripts of the poem have *oure* instead of *youre*, as though Satan were identifying himself with Jewish interests against Christianity.

116. *in an aleye . . . a privee place* The hired murderer is given a suitably murky and obscure dwelling-place.

117. *gan forby for to pace* 'passed by'.

118–9. The murder, described in four bluntly factual clauses, shocks us into seeing the crime in its undisguised ugliness.

120–1. The sense of horror is increased by the revelation that the pit was in fact a common privy. We might wonder why the Prioress does not disclose this at once. She seems to be bent upon rousing strong feelings against the Jews by making the circumstances of the crime even more outrageous. The term *wardrobe* generally meant a small private chamber or dressing-room, but it was also used in this euphemistic way.

120. *they him threwe* The conspirators of line 113 are meant.

121. *Where as thise Jewes* 'where the Jews'. *Thise* is often used familiarly, as when the Wife of Bath refers to 'thise wormes, ne thise motthes, ne thise mites', or when the Franklin recalls 'thise olde gentil Britouns'. Here and in line 177 the term expressed scorn and hatred.

122. *of Herodes al newe* 'composed of second Herods'. The allusion to the slaughtered innocents is now explicit.

123. *What may youre yvel entente yow availle?* 'How can your wicked purpose benefit you?'

124. *mordre wol out* 'murder will be revealed'; a proverbial expression which recurs in *The Nun's Priest's Tale* (see Hussey, l. 286).

125. *And namely ther th'onour of God shal sprede* 'and especially where disclosure of the murder causes men to revere God', who reveals it.

126. *out crieth on* 'calls out upon' in accusation. Compare a similar passage in *The Nun's Priest's Tale* where the friend of a murdered man appeals for justice: 'I crie out on the ministres' (Hussey, l. 277). The idea of blood crying out is borrowed from Genesis 4:10.

127. *O martir* A medieval tradition 'by which any child who resembled the Holy Innocents in youthful martyrdom . . . might be assigned to that blessed company' is mentioned by E. V. Gordon in his edition of *Pearl*, pp. xxv–xxvi. The 'blessed company' is composed of the 144,000 to whom St John refers in Revelation 14:3, 4. See the note below.

128–9. *folwinge evere . . . white Lamb celestial* 'These are they which were not defiled with women, for they are virgins. These are they which follow the Lamb whithersoever he goeth.' Revelation 14:4.

129. *quod she* Different explanations have been offered of this interpolated phrase. There is no need to remind us who is speaking, and the comment distracts attention from the tale. Trevor Whittock believes that Chaucer intended this. 'It is not disturbing enough to break the mood, but just sufficient to cause a fleeting reflection: this is the Prioress's vision, drawn from the Bible, but is it really true?' (*A Reading of the Canterbury Tales*, p. 204.) Other explanations are much simpler. We could suppose that Chaucer was merely filling up the line. The question remains open.

131. *Pathmos* Patmos, an island off the west coast of modern Turkey, where according to Revelation 1:9 St John had his vision, though not necessarily where he wrote his book. The 'seven churches which are in Asia' to whom the book is to be sent (Revelation 1:11), all close to Patmos, help us to understand what the *Asie* of line 36 meant for Chaucer.

131–3. *which seith . . . they ne knewe* The syntax of the sentence seems at fault as it has no main clause. Perhaps we should read 'which seith that they goon', which fits the scansion.

132. *Biforn this Lamb* In fact after him, since they follow. The stanza seems to have given Chaucer trouble. *a song al newe* 'And they sang as it were a new song before the throne'. Revelation 14:3.

133. *flesshly* an adverb qualifying *knewe*, not an adjective.

134–5. *awaiteth . . . after* 'waits for'.

136. *for which* 'for which reason'.

137. *bisy thoght* 'agitated mind'.

139. *she gan so fer espie* 'she discovered this much'.

141. *enclosed* The context seems to require a stronger term than 'shut up'; her frantic feelings are evidently choking her.

144. *By liklihede hir litel child to finde* 'there was some likelihood of finding her son'.

145–6. *evere on Cristes mooder . . . she cride* Her veneration of Christ's mother is suggested by the religious teaching she gives her son; see lines 57–9. A more particular reason for her appealing to the Virgin is that Mary too lost her son, and could be expected to sympathise with other troubled and bereaved mothers.

146. *thus she wroghte* 'she did this'.

147. *Among the cursed Jues she him soghte* The epithet *cursed* is applied to the Jews in lines 118, 122 and 233. Here it may be intended to suggest what an extremity of worry and fear was needed to drive the mother to carry her search into the hateful ghetto itself.

150. *went oght forby* 'went past at all' or, more simply, 'had passed by'.

151. *of his grace* 'mercifully'.

152. *Yaf in hir thoght* 'put it into her mind'. *inwith a litel space* 'shortly afterwards', or 'in a little while'.

153. *she cride* 'she should call'.

155–6. The Prioress recalls her opening theme, 'Out of the mouths of babes and sucklings'.

By mouth of innocentz The 'litel clergeon' is not a babe, though he has now become in effect one of the innocents; and just as those infants 'on the brest soukinge' show forth God's praise without comprehending it, so the praise which comes out of the murdered boy's mouth is still in a tongue which he does not understand.

lo, heere thy might! 'See here your power displayed!'

157–8. *this emeraude . . . the ruby bright* Green and red happen to be the colours of the beads on the Prioress's rosary, normally black. See *The General Prologue*, 158–9.

159. *Ther he* 'where he'.

160. *He* Alma redemptoris *gan to singe* A splendid dramatic touch. In other versions of the story the search is led to the house by the singing. Here it begins as though in response to the

mother's call when she is close at hand, bursting out at the end of the stanza as the sentence approaches its conclusion.

161.   *al the place gan to ringe* An expression familiar from other passages of Chaucer's work. In *The Miller's Tale,* Nicholas plays his 'gay sautrie . . . so sweetly that al the chamber rong' (see Winny ll:105–7). In the present passage it evokes a sense of reverberating sound greater than a small boy's voice could normally produce.

163.   *In coomen for to wondre upon this thing* 'came in to marvel at this happening'.

164.   *the provost* the chief magistrate of the town.

165.   *anon withouten tarying* 'immediately, without delay'. The phrase is tautologous, but repetition emphasises the instant response.

167.   *honour of mankinde* because although a human being, Mary was chosen to bear God's son.

168.   *leet he binde* 'he ordered them to be arrested'. The sequence of his two actions is significant.

170.   *Up taken was* 'was lifted out of the pit', still singing at the top of his voice.

172.   *the nexte abbay* 'an abbey near at hand'. Chaucer is probably thinking of England, where religious houses were plentiful.

173.   *the beere* 'the bier', a stretcher-like framework with legs used for carrying the body to the funeral service and to the grave.

174.   *the peple that was theere* Chaucer regards the collective *peple* as a singular noun.

175.   *newe Rachel* 'second Rachel', referring to Matthew 2:18, 'lamentation, and weeping, and great mourning, Rachel weeping for her children, and would not be comforted, because they are not.' The allusion looks back to Jeremiah 31:15.

177.   *dooth . . . for to sterve* 'sentences to death'.

178.   *and that anon* 'without any delay'.

179.   *He nolde no swich cursednesse observe* 'he refused absolutely to condone such a wicked crime'; another double negative construction. *Nolde* is the contracted form of *ne wolde*, would not.

180. *Yvele shal have that yvele wol deserve* 'wicked deeds shall have their proper punishment'. These criminals are not to expect mercy, though at the end of the tale the Prioress begs God to be merciful to 'we sinful folk'.

181. *wilde hors* 'wild horses'. The singular and plural forms of the noun were the same, as with 'sheep' today. *he dide hem drawe* 'he ordered them to be dragged about'; a process designed to leave the victim bleeding and mutilated, but still alive.

182. *he heng hem by the lawe* 'he caused them to be hanged according to law'. The phrase *by the lawe* suggests, perhaps unintentionally, that the torture was not legally justified.

183. *this beere, this innocent* those previously referred to. *ay* throughout the service.

184. Biforn the chief auter 'in front of the high altar'. Only the bodies of especially venerated persons were allowed to lie in this place. Usually the corpse lay in the nave during the funeral service, or at best within the chancel.

whil masse laste 'throughout mass'.

185. *covent* the body of monks who made up the religious fraternity.

186. *Han sped hem* 'busied themselves'. *ful faste* tautologous after the previous phrase, but the monks may have felt some urgency about burying the boy. An incident in *The Pardoner's Tale* implies that the common people were buried within twenty-four hours of death: see Spearing, lines 378–87.

187. *hooly water* Aspersion, or sprinkling with holy water, is one of the rites of the Roman Catholic funeral service.

188. *yet spak* 'still he continued to sing'. Aspersion might have given his spirit peace and caused the singing to stop.

190. *which that was* 'who was'.

191. *As monkes been – or elles oghte be* Although the Monk among the Canterbury pilgrims, described immediately after the Prioress in *The General Prologue*, is an attractively vital and forthright character, he is a poor churchman and not at all holy. The Prioress

might be mildly reprimanding his spiritual shortcomings, though she herself falls short of perfection in several ways. Alternatively, she may be correcting the slanderous impression left by the previous tale, which describes the cuckolding of a wealthy merchant by a rascally monk. But her comment is not necessarily intended to serve either purpose. In her charming innocence she likes to suppose that monks are pious and devout, as she herself must seem to her own judgement; and if she is half-aware that they are not always so, her mild reproof may be enough to shame them into better behaviour.

193. *I halse thee* Some way must be found of releasing the boy's spirit from a body no longer able to live by natural means. The abbot's questioning is designed to discover how this can be brought about.

194. *In vertu of the hooly Trinitee* The abbot implores the boy 'by the power of the Holy Trinity' to explain the miracle of his continued singing. This solemn adjuration gives weight to his request, and in a form which might compel the boy to answer.

196. *Sith that thy throte is kut to my seminge* 'since, as I think, your throat is cut in two'.

198. *as by wey of kinde* 'according to natural law'.

200. *as ye in bookes finde* 'as you may read in books'. The comment is surprising in a seven-year old who can barely read, though characteristic of Chaucer himself. When books were scarce and information hard to come by, the written word held a special importance.

201. *Wil that his glorie laste* 'wishes his praise to endure'.

205. *as after my konninge* 'to the best of my ability', or 'as well as I knew how'.

206. *whan that I my lyf sholde forlete* 'when I was forced to lose my life' or, more colloquially, 'while I was being killed'. *Sholde* has the force of 'must'.

208. *in my deyinge* 'as I lay dying'.

210. *me thoughte* 'it seemed to me'.

a greyn a small pearl; an appropriate emblem of purity.

211.   *and singe moot certeyn* 'and indeed am compelled to sing'.

213.   *Til fro my tonge of taken is the greyn* 'until the pearl is removed from my tongue'. This is the condition which the abbot wished to discover, so that the boy could yield up his spirit.

218.   *This hooly monk, this abbot, him meene I* The qualification may be ironic: can the audience believe in the existence of a 'hooly monk'? However sceptical they may be, the Prioress insists that the abbot was indeed such a person. But the line may be innocent of any such purpose. 'I'm talking about the abbot, whom I mentioned earlier.'

220.   *And he yaf up the goost* It is, of course, the boy who dies, not the abbot.

223.   *he fil al plat upon the grounde* not falling in a faint, but in reverence both of the miracle which he has witnessed and of the presence of the Virgin, who has just received the boy's soul: see line 215. The brothers follow his example.

224.   *as* 'as if'.

227.   *and forth been went* 'and left the abbey', presumably to prepare a tomb.

231.   *Ther he is now, God leve us for to meete!* 'Wherever he may now be, may God allow us to meet him.'

232.   *Hugh of Lincoln* a boy supposedly murdered by Jews in 1255, but the legend seems to have been current before 1200. If we are to imagine the Prioress as speaking towards the end of the fourteenth century, she must be mistaken in believing that this similar crime – if it took place at all – happened 'but a litel while ago'. Another boy, St William of Norwich, was supposedly crucified by Jews in 1144, but similar tales of atrocity were circulating as early as the fifth century. There is no evidence that any of these allegations against the Jews had any basis in fact, other than the violent antisemitic prejudice which *The Prioress' Tale* itself illustrates. In his *Chaucer Handbook*, R. D. French points out that this folk tradition received fresh impetus during the twelfth

century, when tales of boy martyrs were linked to the flourishing cult of the Virgin Mary, whose miraculous powers either preserved the boy or exposed his murderers.

235. *preye eek for us* By Roman Catholic custom, prayers are addressed not only to God but to saints who may intercede with God on behalf of the sinner. The force of *eek* is 'as we pray to you, do you also pray for us'.

236. *God so merciable* As the closing line shows, the Son and not the Father is meant.

238. *his mooder Marie* The tale is brought appropriately to a close on the name of the blessed Virgin in whose honour it has been told.

Glossary

abbay abbey

accordinge in keeping with

after according to

again against, contrary to

agast frightened, afraid

agon ago

al all, completely

alday always, at any time

aleye alley, back street

alighte alights, settles

al new anew, repeated

always perpetually,
    continuously

amonges amid

anon immediately

antiphoner anthem book

as like, as if

Asie Asia Minor

atte laste at last, eventually

auter altar

availle help, benefit

awaiteth waits for

awey away

ay always

bad bade, told

been went are gone, went

beere bier

ben been

beten beaten, punished

biforn before, in front of

bigan began

binde bind, pinion

biside nearby

bisy worried

boldely confidently, loudly

bringe fro separate from

burien bury, inter

cam passed

carien carry

caste threw

casten thrown

caughte took hold of

cause reason

certes certainly, for sure

certeyn for sure

chastite chastity

childhede childhood

citee city

cleere pure, unblemished

clergeon schoolboy

compaignie company,
    followers

conjure adjure, appeal to

construe translate, interpret

contree country, land

coomen came

covent convent, religious
    community

cride cried, called, appealed
    to

Crist Christ

Cristemasse Christmas

Cristen –e Christian

cursednesse wickedness

dayes lighte daylight

declare explain

dede deed

deere dear, precious

deeth death

despit scorn, contempt

deye die

deyinge dying, death

dide did, showed

dignitee importance, worth

diligence endeavour, earnest
  effort

doctrine teaching,
  instruction

doon do

dooth does, causes

dorste dared

doun downe

draw drag about

drede fear, foreboding

drough drew, moved

dwelte lived

echon each one

eek also, in addition

elles else

elleswhere elsewhere

emeraude emerald

enclosen shut up, inter

encressen increase, add to

entente purpose, intention

entraille bowels

er before

espie discover, find out

evaungelist evangelist

evere always

evere in oon continually

everemo continuously

expounde –n explain

Fadres Father's

faille fail to happen

fare do

fast tight

fecche fetch

felawe friend, companion

fer far

ferther further

fil fell

firste first, original

flesshly carnally, sexually

flour flower

folwinge following

foo enemy

forby by, past

forgat forgot

forlete leave, give up

foule wicked, shameful

fraineth asks, enquires

free noble, gracious (l. 15)
  unobstructed (l. 42)

gan did
  began (l. 161)

gemme gem

getest obtain

glorie praise

gooth goes

goost ghost, Holy Spirit

goost biforn anticipates

goth goes

grammeere Latin

greet great

grete great

greyn seed pearl

gruf face downwards

gydeth guide, direct (polite imperative)

gyden guide, lead

hadde had

halse implore

han have

hastily speedily

Hebraik Hebrew

heeld held

heep crowd

heere here

hem them

heng hanged

hent seized

herde heard

herieth praises

herkned listened to

herte heart

heryinge praise

hevene heaven

image figure, statue

innocentz small children

inwith within, after

Jewerie Jewish quarter, ghetto

Jewes Jews

Jhesu Jesus

Juerie ghetto

Jues Jews'

kan know how to, know

kinde (adj.) compassionate; (sb.) nature, natural law

kitte cut

knele kneel

knewe touched, lay with

knowes knees

konne learn

konning knowledge, skill

koude knew

kut cut, severed

labour endeavour

lamentacioun outcry of grief

langage language

large great

laste lasted (l. 184) endure (l. 201)

laude praise

lawes laws'

leere learn

leet let, allow

lerned studied

lerninge studying, learning

lest likes, pleases

leve grant, allow

leyde laid

liklihede likelihood, probability

litel little

lith lies, remains

lyf life

lucre financial profit

magnificence glory, splendour

maide virgin

maistow can you

maked composed

manere kind of

marbul marble

martir martyr

martirdom martyrdom

masse mass

mateere subject

may can

meete meet

merciable merciful

merveillous wonderful

mighte could

monkes monks

mooder mother

moodres mother's

moot must

mordre murder

Moyses Moses's

multiplie increase

namely especially

namoore no more, nothing else

nat not

naught not, not at all

nay no

ne not

nekke boon neck-bone, spine

ner and ner nearer and nearer

nexte nearest, nearby

noght not

nolde would not

noote tune

notable well known

observe favour, condone

of through, about

of taken taken off, removed

oght at all

pace pass

parfourned fulfilled

parfournest performs, fulfils

Pathmos Patmos

pavement paved or tiled floor

peple people, folk

perced pierced

pitee grief, tenderness

pitous sorrowful

pitously piteously

place dwelling, home

plat flat

poure poor, wretched

precious of great spiritual worth

presence company

preyde asked, begged

preye ask, beg

preyeth appeals

primer book of prayers used to teach children to read

privee secret

prively privately

processioun procession

purgen evacuate, empty out

quod said

ravishedest seized, took possession of

rede read

remembre call to mind

reverence honour, respect

reyn rain

right just

roote root, source

rote, by by heart

salte salt

salue greet, salute

sapience wisdom

Sathanas Satan

saugh saw

science learning

scole school

scoleward on the way to school

seide said

seint saint

sely innocent

seminge judgement

sentence subject, theme

set fixed

seye tell, relate, signify, say

seyn say

shent come to harm, be punished

shewen reveal, declare

sholde should, must

singe —n sing

sith since

smal —e small

socour help, succour

softely gently, without a struggle

soght searched for

somtime sometimes

sone son

song —e sang

soone soon, at once

soukinge sucking

soules souls'

sowded fastened

space short time

spak spoke

sped hurried, busied

sprede spread, be declared

spreynd sprinkled, aspersed

stant stands

sterve die

stinte stop, leave off

stones slabs, blocks

strete street

supposed assumed, believed

susteene sustain, bear

sustened permitted, tolerated

swal swelled

swetnesse sweetness, beauty

swich such

swowning fainting

tarying waiting, delay

teeris tears

tel tell

tendre young, small

thanne then

the thee

theere there

thennes forth from then on

ther there, where
    wherever (l. 231)

therto for that purpose

thilke that

thise these

thoght anxiety, worry (l. 137)
    mind (l. 152)

thoughte seemed

thries three times

throte throat

thurgh through

thurghout from end to end,
    throughout

thyn thine

tonge tongue

tooken took

torment torture

trikled trickled, fell

Trinitee Trinity

twelf twelve

twies twice

unbrent unconsumed, not
    burned

unnethes hardly, scarcely

unstable changeable,
    unsteady

upright face upwards

usage custom

used practised

usure usury, money-lending
    at interest

wardrobe privy

waspes wasps'

wayk weak, feeble

wel well

welle spring, fountain

wende go, pass

went gone, past

weye way

weye, by the along the road

what when

which who

whos whose

widwes widow's

wil desire, wishes

wiste knew, understood

withouten without

wol will, wish to

wolde would

wondre marvel

wone habit, custom

wordes words

worship honour, reverence

worthiness excellence

wroghte did

wroot wrote

yaf gave, set

ybounde tied up

ycomen come, born

ye yea, yes

yeer, yere year

ykorven cut open

yong young

yow you

ysprad spread

ytake taken, removed

yvel evil

CPSIA information can be obtained
at www.ICGtesting.com
Printed in the USA
LVHW080329280720
661628LV00004B/262